Beyond Violence

Empowering Black Youth Autonomy

Alyssa Mileham

ABSTRACT

Through this book I sought to add to the literature regarding the influence of pervasive police brutality on young Black people. In it I explore the relationship between police brutality and influence on Black people's bodily autonomy by gender, gender identity, and sexuality. Through the lenses of Afro-Pessimism and Intersectionality, I find that the pervasive culture of police violence influences the bodily autonomy of young Black people. This influence varies by gender, gender identity, and sexuality, mirroring the policing of Black people's bodies throughout history. As such, I advocate for structural change in policing such that young Black people can self-autonomize and self-actualize as full human beings whose lives matter and have independent meaning.

TABLE OF CONTENTS

Chapter 1: Introduction

FORMULATION OF THE PROBLEM

The Black Lives Matter movement began in 2012 with a love letter to Black people written by co-founder of the movement, Alicia Garza, after the murder of Trayvon Martin, a seventeen year old Black child, and the acquittal of his vigilante murderer, George Zimmerman (Ransby 2018). This set of events underscored in Black communities the degree to which their lives did not matter – that it was fine for them to be followed and murdered and that there were no consequences for assailants. The result echoed Judge Taney's opinion in the *Dred Scott* decision, that Black people were "so far inferior that they had no rights which the White man was bound to respect" (*Dred Scott v. Sanford* 1857: 407). By contrast, in the letter Garza asserted that "Black lives matter" which later became the slogan for the movement that followed.

It is important to note the larger socio-political context that surrounded Trayvon Martin's murder. Martin was killed just before Barack Obama's re-election after four years of his presidency (Ransby 2018). In light of protests in the wake Trayvon Martin's death, the Malcom X Grassroots movement released a well-researched report entitled "Operation Ghetto Storm," named after the US Desert Storm military invasion of Iraq of the same name, which detailed that a Black person was killed by police, security guards, or vigilantes every twenty-eight hours (Ransby 2018). The *Washington Post* and other public entities began researching this statistic further uncovering police violence and, "the presence of a clear pattern and a disturbing uptick of incidents across the country" (Ransby 2018: 32).

Two years later, after the onset of the Black Lives Matter movement and the murder of Trayvon Martin, Michael Brown, an unarmed eighteen-year-old Black child, was murdered in 2014 by a police officer. His deceased body was then left out on the street in his neighborhood exposed for hours (Ransby 2018). Officer Darren Wilson later testified that Brown "looked like a demon" during his interaction with him and a friend over walking in the street (Ransby 2018: 48). This implies that his guilt lay in his personhood or lack thereof and not the minor altercation at the convenience store later cited by the officer (Ransby 2018). He was not just a high school kid with an attitude but a "demon." Michael Brown's death, and his humanity being taken in leaving his lifeless body in the street, kicked the Black Lives Matter movement into overdrive through the Ferguson protests that followed. Witnesses stated that Brown was in a surrendering position when murdered, sparking the protest slogan, "hands up, don't shoot." Temple University professor and political commentator Marc Lamont Hill asserted that Black boys and men like Brown had societally been given the title of "nobody" and "to be nobody means to be considered disposable" (Ransby 2018: 50). I assert that this status as "nobody" also means a lack of humanity and in turn a lack of the right to bodily autonomy.

In this thesis I analyze the way in which Black people across genders and sexualities shape their bodily autonomy in response to witnessing police violence in the news and social media, Black Lives Matter protests, and Black people's own face-to-face encounters with police, including police violence. Like Mallik (2017) I assert as my hypothesis that Black people do not have control over their bodily autonomy because police brutality and state violence are constant looming threats to them. As such, young Black people may self-govern to avoid the violence that institutionalized racism permits instead of governing their bodies in dignified manners in accordance with their own free will. The result would be a community disenfranchised, dehumanized, ununified intra communally, and lacking bodily autonomy. Here, I define bodily autonomy as "the right to self-governance over one's body without external influence or coercion" (Blanco, 2018). My research questions are: Do young Black people feel they have bodily autonomy in interactions with the police under the threat of police brutality, and what can this reveal about their everyday lives? How does this experience vary by gender, gender identity and/or sexuality? This study is needed because it adds to our knowledge regarding the ways in which Black bodily autonomy is impacted by the pervasiveness of police violence. It also explores the differential influence of that violence on young Black people's gender, gender identity and/or sexuality and give voice to those multiply minoritized by sex, gender and/or sexuality within the Black community.

Theoretical Foundations

During this thesis I used the theories of Afro-Pessimism and Intersectionality to frame the findings regarding young Black people's understandings of bodily autonomy (Wilderson et al. 2017; Collins and Bilge 2020). Afro-Pessimism "is a reoriented understanding of the composition of slavery: instead of being defined as a relation of (forced) labor, it is more accurately thought of as a relation of property" (Wilderson et al. 2017: 8). Intersectionality theory critically advances the argument that people can have multiple marginalized social locations, privileged social locations, and a combination of both (Collins and Bilge 2020).

From an Afro-pessimist's perspective, Black people effectively are socially dead, deprived of the essence of their humanity. By social death, Afro-pessimist scholars mean Black people have no recognizable social rights which renders them "1) open to gratuitous violence, as opposed to violence contingent upon some transgression or crime; 2) natally alienated, their ties of birth not recognized and familial structures intentionally broken apart; and 3) generally dishonored, or disgraced before any thought or action is considered" (Wilderson et al. 2017: 8). Here, one and three are most apropos to this study. Taking the latter first, Black people are regarded as without honor, inherently suspect, and criminal (Brooms and Clark 2020; Carbado 2017). This means generalized fear and anxiety among young Black people when it comes to police and policing (Smith Lee and Robinson 2019) resulting in significant negative mental health outcomes (Jindal et al.. 2021) because they do feel that they are generally vulnerable to violence from the police. Through exposure to pervasive police violence in the news and social media, in addition to what participants experience directly with the police, they are aware that they are vulnerable to police violence and that the police can do whatever they want to their bodies without consequence. The outcome of the Derek Chauvin, a police officer with a history of reported complaints and accusations of brutality, case is the exception which proves the rule (Eligon et al. 2021). Chauvin's indifference to George Floyd's life is captured on video as Chauvin chokes Floyd to death using the unauthorized technique of leaning his knee on Floyd's neck for nearly nine minutes. Chauvin's conviction happens because Floyd's death is not instant and Chauvin had opportunities to cease deadly force. In other cases where deadly force is administered quickly, like from a bullet, or indirectly, through negligent securing of a Black body in a police vehicle, police officers tend not be convicted for their violent and/ or negligent behavior (Levenson 2021). From the murders of Michael Brown to Freddie Gray and beyond, police tend to be exonerated for killing Black people. The lack of accountability lends to a sense of Black people's disposability.

During slavery, Black people's very beings were commodified, not just their labor, and this eliminated Black people from the category of social subjects and thus humanity (Wilderson et al. 2017; Ponton 2016). However, post-emancipation, Black people's bodies were still subjected to White control through violence and the police state (Alexander 2010). Absent access to the basic rights of humanity to be, Black people are "1) open to gratuitous violence, as opposed to violence contingent upon some transgression or crime; 2) natally alienated, their ties

of birth not recognized and familial structures intentionally broken apart; and 3) generally

dishonored, or disgraced before any thought or action is considered" (Wilderson et al. 2017: 8).

Ontologically speaking, this means that Black people exist for their oppressors which is different

than being an exploited or oppressed person, someone with a degree of humanity, who are,

"object(s) of accumulation and fungibility (exchangeability)" (Wilderson et al. 2017: 8).

This legacy of the subjugation of blackness was carried into the 21st century into every

part of our society, including the institutions of justice and law enforcement (Alexander 2010).

Even Black police officers are not safe from fellow White police officers. Thus, in the case

where a plain-clothed White officer with his peers shoots another approaching plain-clothed

officer who happens to be Black and that Black cop's lawyer laments that he was "treated as an

ordinary Black guy on the street," there is a fundamental problem with the devaluation of

Blackness (Wilderson et al. 2017: v). As such, we must go beyond simple analysis of police

behavior and reform and instead we must confront the roots of the problem, which are racism,

white supremacy, and dehumanization (Wilderson et al. 2017: v; Ponton 2016). Afro-Pessimism

seeks to do the work of going beyond by shifting the proverbial focus away from centering

whiteness, and White people, and instead on social-subjecthood and the paradigm of Black vs

non-Black (Wilderson et al. 2017).

In addition to Afro-Pessimism, I used Intersectionality to analyze differences in Black

people's access to bodily autonomy by gender, sex, and sexual orientation. Intersectionality

theory seeks to identify how this phenomenon impacts specific subgroups according to their

multiple social locations, examples being Black women or Black queer folks. According to

Collins and Bilge (2020: 2), the following is an operational definition of Intersectionality: "in a given society at a given time, power relations of race, class, and gender, for example, are not discrete and mutually exclusive entities, but rather build on each other and work together; and that, while often invisible, these intersecting power relations affect all aspects of the social world." In this way I am able to see how participants' intersectional social locations impacted access to their bodily autonomy in police interactions because of how their other social locations intersect with being Black (Mallik 2017; Collins and Bilge 2020; Wilderson et al. 2017).

Kimberlé Crenshaw, the creator of the term "Intersectionality," describes Intersectionality as "an analytic concept to address the complex latent power relations that shape the lives of women of color, and Black women in particular" (Haynes et al. 2020: 752). Crenshaw exemplifies one of the ideas of Intersectionality through the analysis of the court case *DeGraffenreid v General Motors* in which five Black women sued the company for discrimination against Black women. Their claims of sexism and racism were dismissed because the company employed white women and Black men. What the courts failed to consider was the intersections of Black women's specific social locations. Black women experience racism and sexism simultaneously as they experience the world as both people who are Black and women (Crenshaw 1989). According to multiplicative identity theory, Intersectionality refers to the way in which inequality is institutionalized and thus becomes a part of our structural systems. This is very impactful for people with differential social locations who are affected by inequalities in multiple ways. As such, to fully address social inequity one must approach social problems intersectionally (Wing 1991). Intersectionality is the idea that people can simultaneously be oppressed and the oppressor, someone can have privilege and in other areas of their life be without privilege. Patricia Hill Collins has furthered Intersectionality theory, after shaping it early on, by adding terms like "interlocking systems" and "matrix of domination" which consider the societal conditions one must exist in according to their intersectional identities (Collins 2000; Collins and Bilge 2020). It is important to recognize these intersections so that we can adequately understand them. When interviewing my participants, I asked them intersectional questions concerning their social locations and police brutality.

Patricia Hill Collins and Sirma Bilge define Intersectionality as "investigat[ing] how intersecting power relations influence social relations across diverse societies as well as individual experiences in everyday life" (2020: 2). This means that,

> In a given society at a given time, power relations of race, class, and gender, for example, are not mutually exclusive entities, but rather build on each other and work together; and that, while often invisible, these intersecting power relations affect all aspects of the social world.

This idea that power relations regarding intersectional social locations are not mutually exclusive is very important because it can lead to understanding the power relations that Black men, for example, endure because in the public sphere Black men do not receive patriarchal privilege. This is specifically because their manhood exists with their Blackness. For Black men patriarchal power only exists within the Black community, in which power relations are even more complicated. This framework of understanding power relations helps us to challenge our long held beliefs about *how* people are privileged especially those with intersecting social locations.

It is also important to consider Intersectionality theory's roots in Black feminism. In doing so we can see how the theory parallels the works of authors and academics such as bell hooks in her quest to understand why Black women endure "sexist, racist, and classist oppression" by analyzing all of their intersectional social locations in comparison to their more privileged white counterparts who also occupy intersectional social locations (hooks 1984).

Through the analyzing of intersectional social locations by Black feminists like bell hooks we also find the origins of ideas such as the matrix of domination through how hooks conceptualizes power relations in conjunction with Intersectionality. Hooks' work can be seen as using Intersectionality theory through the critical praxis lens, particularly in her endeavors toward social change. Hooks has also chastised early white feminism for essentially not being intersectional, arguing that the most marginalized women's needs must be met first by advocating for resources such as government funded day care centers and by including the discussion of class struggle in feminist efforts (hooks 1984). This intersectional feminism envisioned by hooks also discouraged individualism because she noted that women's individual successes, such as climbing the ladder in male dominated career fields, do not equate to the advancement of the feminist movement. Instead the feminist movement only advances when the needs of all women are met (hooks 1984).

Throughout my study I use Intersectionality theory as critical praxis to call attention to how we commonly conceptualize issues such as police brutality and bodily autonomy as separate from each other due to society's inability to see how these issues impact marginalized people with intersecting social locations (Collins and Bilge 2020: 40). The critical praxis perspective also encourages academics to go beyond simply understanding in order to actively solve social problems, making understanding Intersectionality theory from the critical praxis perspective important to social justice work (Collins and Bilge 2020: 50). This is because it requires one to use their knowledge to navigate everyday actions. In using this perspective there can exist an intersection between academia and social justice. Critical inquiry is also used to imagine intersectional frameworks such as the ones studied in this thesis.

One threat to Intersectionality as an overarching idea is the neoliberalism of the masses which seeks to depoliticize the theory (Bilge 2013). Here, the continued flow of money into the economy, and thus the pockets of our most wealthy, take precedence over everything else even outside of fields centered around the economy. Under neoliberalism, Intersectionality is depoliticized and instead becomes a marketing tool or a misunderstood catch-all for identity politics. Neoliberalism and its free market perspective create a bastardized Intersectionality in which the goal is no longer to meet the needs of our society's most marginalized and instead can become diluted into just diversity quotas for corporations who want to seem progressive while also making money (Bilge 2013).

Collins also describes apathy towards people of different marginalized identities than oneself as another threat to Intersectionality (Ore and Collins 2022). Echoing Audre Lorde, Patricia Collins asserts that confronting "that piece of the oppressor which is planted deep within each of us" is vital to any intersectional social change (Lorde 2019:123). Specifically, Collins argues that intersectional groups who have both marginalized and privileged social locations particularly have difficulty in identifying that piece of the oppressor in themselves. One example of this that Collins provides is radical leftists who believe class solidarity would end racism and misogyny. They believe this because they often can only relate to being marginalized by class and not by their race or gender. To overcome this social dilemma, Collins postulates that we must ask new questions. These questions must be framed around the dichotomy of domination and subordination instead of forcing groups of multi-faceted people into the dichotomous idea that they are either the oppressor or the privileged instead of accepting socially and personally that one can be both (Ore and Collins 2022). These questions include the following: "How are relationships of domination and subordination structured and maintained in the American political economy? How do race, class, and gender function as parallel and interlocking systems that shape this basic relationship of domination and subordination (Ore and Collins 2022: 485)?

It is also important to note that while one's bodily autonomy is limited in our society according to their intersectional social locations one can still have the ability to assert agency within this limited framework. Though Black people of varying other social locations have a constrained access to agency, they still have the agency to operate within that constrained agency. Intersectionality theory is adding to ideas about social stratification in a way that reconceptualizes how we think about our social locations (Collins and Bilge 2020).

My study is needed due to its contribution to the empirical research literature regarding Black people and police brutality. It also is needed because understanding Intersectionality theory can in part help to address issues like the limitations on Black bodily autonomy due to the pervasive threat of police violence both real and perceived. This is done through integrating intersectional approaches into the theory of Afro-Pessimism.

Intersectionality and Bodily Autonomy

The following is a continuation of the formulation of the root problem this thesis seeks to address. It is done while also addressing the intersectionality of the problem as well.

Black Women and Bodily Autonomy

Black women's bodily autonomy is constrained in a state of pervasive police violence. This is because as Black people they are vulnerable to police violence and police brutality (Embrick 2015; Schwartz, 2020; Threadcraft 2017) and because they are both Black *and* women that they are vulnerable to sexual violence by the police (Ponton 2016; Ritchie and Jones-Brown

2017). They are persecuted by the police in particular ways because they are both Black and women. Their blackness is not separate from their womanhood and their womanhood is not separate from their blackness (Sarkisian 2020).

An example of this is the case of former Officer Daniel Holtzclaw, who sexually assaulted eighteen Black women while on duty because he believed, and admitted, that he thought no one would care specifically because they were Black women (Sankofa 2016). Yet the targeting of Black women precisely because of the gender and/or gender identity are largely invisible to society at large (Ritchie 2017). While most Americans can with ease recall the names of Black men killed by police, Black women's names were largely ignored in the media and were often quickly forgotten. Kimberlé Crenshaw's Ted Talk on the Say Her Name campaign thrust some national attention to the fact that Black women experience police violence (Gomez 2021).

Black women are subject to violence in this way not only because they are not perceived to be human because of their blackness, but also because they are not seen as feminine, ideal women, because of their race (Collins 2000). In their study of Black women subjected to police raids, Greene and colleagues (2021) found that Black women perceived police to regard them through stereotyped lenses. Thus, as Black women navigate their bodily autonomy with police, they perform gender in ways to make themselves more safe – deploying femininity as a protective shield (Greene et al.. 2021).

Black Men and Bodily Autonomy

Black men's bodily autonomy is constrained because they are extremely vulnerable to police brutality and are funneled into prisons for free labor (Mallik 2017; Chaney and Robertson

2013; Embrick 2015). This is in conjunction with the fact that our capitalist state benefits in many ways from Black men's subjugation. The school-to-prison pipeline serves as a continuation of slavery in which Black men are disenfranchised for state capitalist endeavors and their free labor (Alexander 2010; Cooper 2015).

The application of Intersectionality theory is an important framework for analyzing Black men's access to bodily autonomy. Interestingly, Black men having both social locations of being Black and also being men is what leaves them so vulnerable to police and state violence even though being men is a social location of privilege. It is important to note that outside of the Black community, much of the *institutional* privileges that come with being men do not apply to Black men. Black men are also less educated, on average, than their female counterparts, who are the most educated group in America (Porter and Bronzaft 1995). This can, in part, be explained by the school-to-prison pipeline and America's high rate of recidivism (Cooper 2015). In America, many Black men do not have a chance to succeed, especially if they were born into an underprivileged community that lacks resources for its public schools. In these kinds of schools, school resource officers have a large presence. This means that situations such as school fights, which are typically left on the playground, at white public schools with less or no officers, are escalated to criminal charges (Pigott, Stearns, and Khey, 2018). Black children are not given the benefit of the doubt in the same way that their white counterparts are when it comes to authority figures like teachers and these school resource officers. This means that a Black boy's criminal record can begin in childhood making him seem less innocent as an adult should he have any more dealings with the courts. Also, being labeled a felon removes any chance of upward mobility for anyone trying to better themselves after completing their sentence. People with felonies notoriously have a very hard time finding work and their status as a felon bars them from social welfare benefits such as housing and food assistance (Williams, Wilson, and Bergeson, 2019). There are limited means for felons and prison involved persons to survive for these people except by criminal means, which contributes to America's high rate of recidivism (Alper et al.. 2018; Harding et al.. 2017).

The Black Queer Community and Bodily Autonomy

Black queer people's sense of bodily autonomy is impacted by a pervasive state of police violence. This is because in addition to being Black people, generally vulnerable to police violence, as queer people they are subject to sexual assault and police brutality because of their sexuality and/or gender identity (Heberle et al.. 2020; Krieger 2020; Embrick 2015; Schwartz 2020). Here, as a queer identified person, I am using the term queer as an umbrella to encompass all who identify as lesbian, gay, bisexual, transgender, queer, questioning, intersex, pansexual, 2-spirited, asexual and allies (Maniago 2018). Black queer people are perceived criminally not just because of their Blackness but also their sexuality and/or gender identity (Leighton 2018). Under the gaze of police, they are subject to further dehumanization through misgendering and ridicule (Ellison 2019; Ritchie 2017). Also, queer Black folks must contend with their intersectional social locations because they are both Black and queer. They face violence, which results in a lack of bodily autonomy, from both of their socially stratified communities, the Black community and the LGBT community, as well as police and state violence (Heberle et al.. 2020; Ritchie and Jones-Brown 2017).

For queer Black people, the loss of bodily autonomy can look like Black trans women having a mortality rate of thirty-five years of age due to violence from the police and their community (CDC 2015). Black trans women perfectly, and tragically, epitomize what it is to have intersectional social locations. They simultaneously are ignored, dehumanized, and even brutalized societally, by police, Black people, non-transgender LGBT folks (Serpe and Nadal 2017; Ponton 2016; Schwartz 2020; Ritchie and Jones-Brown 2017).

The application of Intersectionality theory is an important framework for analyzing Black queer folks' access to their bodily autonomy. They endure feelings of persecution because they are both Black and queer. Their blackness is not separate from their queerness and their queerness is not separate from their blackness. The discrimination that people are subject to with these social locations are not separate from each other. Also, the intersectional way Black queer people experience racism and homophobia can differ depending on their other social locations (Meyer 2016:143). For example, though Black gay men and Black lesbians may face similar marginalizations, Black lesbians are more likely to face sexual assault than their gay male counterparts. This is furthered when social class is considered because without resources low-income Black lesbians find it hard to leave abusive relationships especially when they have children whom they may fear could be harmed (Meyer 2016: 143). Low-income Black gay men however, face violence in group homes and homeless shelters. Both of these circumstances are often further agitated by familial rejection and even violence which can be more negatively impactful than violence outside of these relationships (Meyer 2016 143).

In sum, police brutality and violence looks differently for different Black people depending on their sex, sexuality and gender identity. However, the result of the fear created by this pervasive violence is the same: a loss of bodily autonomy (Serpe and Nadal 2017).

Overview of the Research

To explore the research question of whether Black people of intersectional social locations feel they have bodily autonomy in interactions with the police under the threat of police brutality and what can this reveal about their everyday lives, I interviewed 15 Black, college-educated, young adults between the ages of 20 and 27. I selected this sample using an equal representation strategy so that the voices would be inclusive of Black people across sex, gender, and sexuality identities.

Using Afro-Pessimism and Intersectionality I found that for Black women respondents, their lack of bodily autonomy in interactions with the police came from societal stereotypes about them having attitudes and being less feminine. Dark-skinned Black women in particular had to contend with how these stereotypes translated to the lack of innocence that comes with femininity in their lives including in interactions with the police. This limited their bodily autonomy to trying not to be perceived in accordance with these stereotypes during these interactions for fear of police retaliation. Black men suffered the most from a lack of bodily autonomy in interactions with police. During the course of the interviews, a phenomenon that came to be referred to as "walking with a purpose" was an experience many of the Black male respondents identified with. Walking with a purpose included Black men going from casually walking in the public sphere to walking as if they had somewhere to be when in the presence of police. It also included not wearing hoodies and other clothing commonly worn by Black people. These men learned how to do so at very young ages from older Black men in their lives. They also expressed that they had to do this specifically because they were both Black and men due to Black masculinity being stereotyped as deviant in society. In a sense, during these interactions with police Black men were not self-governing their bodies and instead were being governed by institutionalized anti-Blackness. For many of the men, this even became a part of their identities as they grew older while interacting with police over the years. For Black trans masculine respondents, the lack of bodily autonomy they experienced in interactions with the police was the gender dysphoria they experienced when police misgendered them and they didn't feel allowed to correct them. Some of these respondents indicated that they also were afraid of police gendering them as masculine because of how the police interact with Black men. They also noted that safety for Black women was also not guaranteed due to their seeming disposability in society.

Chapter 2: REVIEW OF THE LITERATURE

Much empirical research on police brutality and Black people's experiences with police brutality have been undertaken. This literature review focuses on earlier academic and research studies that helped me contextualize my research on the impact of police violence on Black people's sense of bodily autonomy across sex, gender, and sexuality.

In *Racism and Police Brutality in America,* authors Chaney and Robertson seek to answer two questions: What, if any, changes have occurred in the nation's police departments 21 years after the Rodney King beating and how does the general public perceive police and how does race and racism shape this discourse? To find the answers to these questions the authors analyzed survey data provided by the National Police Misconduct Statistics and Reporting Project (NPMSRP). The researchers found that between the months of April 2019 to June 2010 there were 5,986 reports of misconduct, 382 fatalities linked to misconduct, and settlements and judgments that totaled $347,455,000 (Chaney and Robertson 2013).

The researchers discovered four emergent themes in the NPMSRP data using grounded theory: contempt for law enforcement, suspicion of law enforcement, law enforcement as agents of brutality, and respect for law enforcement (Chaney and Robertson 2013). The most prevalent theme was law enforcement as agents of brutality, which was voiced by sixteen of the thirty-six Black contributors, making it the most popular theme, followed by suspicion of law enforcement, respect for law enforcement, and contempt for law enforcement in that order (Chaney and Robertson 2013). This small study implies that Black Americans' feelings about law enforcement is more complicated than much of mainstream media would like to believe. What is unclear here is how this brutality affects Black Americans and perceptions of their bodily autonomy. I used these researchers' framing to shape my research questions and data analysis.

Gottchalk (2012) analyzes the prison sentences of 61 police officers convicted of police brutality in Norway. The author found a significant correlation with more brutality by police officers equating to shorter prison sentences (Gottchalk 2012). This correlation of more brutality resulting in a shorter sentence for the police is striking. Though the study was done in Norway the study is relevant in its conceptualization of the police. Gottchalk also found a significant correlation where "more personal benefit led to a longer jail sentence for police officers" (2012: 509). It is interesting to see that more brutality did not warrant longer sentences, but personal benefits or motivations of the officers did. It is also important to remember that although this study is on convicted police officers, most police officers are not convicted.

Another important facet of police brutality and Black Lives Matter literature is the case of *Graham vs Conner*. Authors Obasogie and Newman studied the impact that the 1989 Graham vs Conner case decision had on the nature of police excessive force claims in federal courts. In this case the Supreme Court enforced that the Fourth Amendment was the only avenue in which courts could handle police brutality claims (Obasogie and Newman 2018). The Fourth Amendment prevents unreasonable search and seizures. The authors found that before the *Graham v Conner* case the courts only used the Fourth Amendment 28% of the time and 90% after (Obasogie and Newman 2018). Before *Graham v Conner*, the Fourteenth Amendment was brought up more than the Fourth Amendment at 40%. Thus, it is reasonable to suggest that the courts changed the course of these court cases. The Fourth Amendment individualized and color-blinded each case separate from larger discussions of racism within our societal institutions unlike the Fourteenth Amendment or its Equal Protection Clause, which prohibits any State from denying a person within its jurisdiction equal protections of the laws. The authors conclude that the court's perception of how the public ought to conceive and bind the relationship between the constitution and a victim of police brutality's civil rights to be free from the state.

Helms and Costanza seek to add to the literature on police brutality which they say is "replete with studies focused on individual characteristics and situational exigencies" (Helms and Costanza 2019: 43). In seeking a structural approach to assess alternative explanations, researchers found that "race, criminal violence, and general conditions of economic inequality are strong predictors of police killings of citizens across 3,081 US counties" (Helms and Costanza 2019: 43).

The researchers found that members of Hispanic and African American communities were significantly more likely to be killed by police (Helms and Costanza 2019; Embrick 2015). They also found evidence of lower socioeconomic class being a factor in police brutality (Helms and Costanza 2019). Being a racial minority is predictive of killings. Violent crime offenses and drug arrest rates are both predictors of police killings also (Helms and Costanza 2019).

The authors explain that one unwritten rule of policing is that police demand more respect than they give (Helms and Costanza 2019). "Since police officers are tasked with the actions of street level enforcement, their perceptions of social antagonism and direct hostility readily translate into an aggressive sensibility that tips the balance in favor of force when tensions are rising" (Helms and Costanza 2019: 62). The authors also note that if we insist on police reform, we must abandon efforts rooted in a case-by-case analysis and management of police behavior because instead we should be focusing on telling the truth about the intersectional inequalities of our society (Helms and Costanza 2019).

In "Police killings and their spillover effects on the mental health of Black Americans: bodily autonomy population-based, quasi-experimental study," the authors seek to explore and understand any mental health impacts of police brutality, even if the people impacted are not directly involved (Bor et al. 2018: 302). This psychological study is relevant because it confirms the negative impacts to the Black communities' mental health. I assert that one reason for this negative impact is the loss of bodily autonomy. The study was population-based and quasi-experimental concerning police killings data along with individual level data from the 2013-15 US Behavioral Risk Factor Surveillance System (BRFSS) (Bor et al.. 2018). The findings showed that a little over a third of the 103,710 Black American respondents were exposed to one or more police killings of unarmed Black people in their state within the past threezero to two weeks of poor mental health with the largest negative impacts to mental health occurring one to two months after the incident. The researchers found that police brutality against and killings of unarmed Black people has adverse effects on the Black population's mental health (Bor et al.. 2018).

In *Policing Race, Gender, and Sex: A Review of Law Enforcement Policies* Ritchie and Jones-Brown (2017: 29) surveyed thirty-six police agencies across America and found that, "All departments examined had a policy banning racial profiling. Fewer than a quarter prohibited profiling based on gender, gender identity, or sexual orientation. Although departments generally had a policy explicitly prohibiting sexual harassment and misconduct among employees, more than half had no policy explicitly prohibiting police sexual misconduct against members of the public." This shows how police agencies are unprepared to, and violently so, dignify those with marginalized social locations by considering their intersectionlities and how they can be made vulnerable to abuse because of their marginalizations. Black women are vulnerable to sexual assault by the police thanks to this lack of consideration and Black queer folks become targets of the police when they become unhoused as a result of family homophobia. An example of this is the case of former Officer Daniel Holtzclaw, who sexually assaulted eighteen Black women while on duty because he believed, and admitted, that he thought no one would care specifically because they were Black women (Sankofa, 2016). Yet the targeting of Black women precisely because of the gender and/or gender identity are largely invisible to society at large (Ritchie 2017). Black queer people are also another group within the Black community who face police violence without as much public awareness as their Black male peers. For Black queer people, their encounters with the police typically stem from a lack of support, and sometimes even violence, from their families due to their queer identities.

The current state of literature concerning Black bodily autonomy and police brutality supports the notion that police brutality against Black Americans is a pressing issue (Krieger 2020; Embrick 2015; Schwartz 2020). What is missing from this literature is a more in-depth exploration of the bodily autonomy aspect of this conversation concerning Black people not owning their own bodies in relation to police brutality. I added this to the literature by conducting interviews with Black people of varying backgrounds and discussing with them how police brutality makes them feel about being Black and owning themselves. I also analyzed answers for differences among different socially stratified Black people such as being queer, women, and men. The literature regarding Black women and Black queer people as it pertains to Police brutality is peripheral. By this I mean that Black men remain the primary subject of police brutality in research studies. This is starkly seen in the difference in political reaction regarding the murder of George Floyd which, in the words of his very young daughter, "changed the world" versus the murders of Breonna Taylor or any of the many Black trans women murdered every year which receive(d) no political justice. Research studies also reflect this. What is included in the literature is qualitative analysis of Black women's vulnerability to sexual assault by police and Black queer folks' societal exile from their homophobic and transphobic families and their societally lost personhood under the weight of what it means to be Black queer people.

Chapter 3: RESEARCH METHOD

I used a general qualitative research approach to understand how young Black people navigate their bodily autonomy under the pervasive threat of police violence (Merriam and Tisdell 2015). In this section I provide an overview of my sampling frame, instrumentation, and data analysis. This study was reviewed and approved by the Institutional Review Board at East Carolina University.

Sampling Frame

I interviewed 15 Black young adults and used a combination of purposeful sampling techniques to obtain a diverse representation across genders and sexual orientations/identities. I interviewed five heterosexual females, five heterosexual males, and five queer individuals. I chose to interview 15 people because it is a round number that can be divided evenly amongst my diverse sample and 20 could not be divided evenly. I explained my sampling method to those whom I recruited, in case they questioned why I was asking about sexual orientation / identity. I also asked how each individual predominantly identifies regarding sexual orientation, given that research indicates that a growing number of those who identify as heterosexual also have same-sex relationship experiences. Although this division resulted in a majority who are heterosexual, I purposefully oversampled the proportion of the general population that identifies as queer. All participants were between the ages of 20-27 and all were former or current students of various universities in North Carolina because of my access to them. I used convenience sampling and snowball sampling as a means to find these participants. I gave participants pseudonyms to protect confidentiality. I then transcribed the interviews and coded them for common themes regarding Black people's relationships to their bodily autonomy and social locations. I analyzed the data after transcription for both negative and positive impacts to their bodily autonomy

through the lenses of both Afro-Pessimism and Intersectionality theory.

I also analyzed the relevance of each person's social locations for any impact for or

against their bodily autonomy. I asked respondents for their interpretations of whether their

intersectional locations affected their bodily autonomy. I also analyzed the responses for patterns

across the groups, such as comparing Black men that identify as heterosexual with Black men

who identify as gay. This allowed me to discuss the relevance of Intersectionality in bodily

autonomy and the community-based solutions for these violations of bodily autonomy. My

interview protocol is in the appendix.

The time period in which these interviews took place should also be noted as they took

place during and after Derek Chauvin's trial for the murder of George Floyd, a case that sparked

protests in all fifty of the United States as well as many protests abroad. This case brought

additional topical salience during the interviewing process. Participants cited this case their

interviews.

Instrumentation

Prior to each interview, I reviewed informed consent forms and shared with participants

what they could expect during their interview. In addition, they were informed that they could

opt out of participation at any time including during the interview. I asked each participant a

series of questions pertaining to their bodily autonomy in response to reports of police brutality

or to their own experience with brutality. These questions sought to analyze which of each

participant's social locations positively and negatively impacted each participant's perception of

their bodily autonomy. I recorded interviews by using both note-taking and the Microsoft Teams record feature. After the interview, I also took the time to debrief with participants for their emotional wellbeing.

Data Analysis

After the interviews I transcribed the interviews using the Microsoft Teams recording feature. I began my analysis with a description of each of the participants' demography and social location. I then analyzed these interviews using Afro-Pessimism and Intersectionality to uncover young Black people's feelings of and about bodily autonomy under the pervasiveness of the threat of policy violence. I coded individual questions as well as cross-coded questions.

Next, I used an emergent coding schema. Utilizing my notes and transcripts, I used a constant comparative approach to identify patterns which I distilled into themes. I specifically looked over all of the data I collected and found similarities in participant experiences and feelings and then analyzed these similarities. I present results in the following section.

I also included closed-ended and open-ended questions. Closed-ended questions tended to be demographic or social such as asking each participant how old they were or what their pronouns were. Open ended questions were much more likely to be centered on the participants'' feelings regarding public police brutality cases, for example, or their personal experiences with police and other authority figures. I also used deductive and inductive coding by using Intersectionality theory and Afro-Pessimism theory to analyze my data. I used simple frequencies and cross tabs, for closed-ended questions, to see if there was a relationship between gender and sexual orientation as it pertained to their responses as Black people.

Chapter 4: FINDINGS

In this section I report findings from my research inquiry. I used emergent themes as shaped by understandings of Afro-Pessimism and Intersectionality to understand how young Black people navigate their bodily autonomy in relation to a state of pervasive police violence and how those strategies vary by sex, gender identity, and sexuality. Appendix B includes an overview of the interviews as well as descriptions of the participants.

Trust the police?

I begin with the responses to the closed-ended questions in order to unveil my participants' feelings toward police. I used the following closed-ended question derived from Chaney and Robertson (2013) to gauge participants' attitudes towards police: "Which phrase best fits your feelings or perceptions of police?" The available responses to this question were five phrases as follows: "Contempt or hatred for law enforcement", "suspicion of law enforcement", "view law enforcement as agents of systematic and institutional brutality", "respect for law enforcement", and "indifference to the police". Most participants could not choose just one phrase because one did not encompass the fullness of their perspectives regarding law enforcement. Over the course of all fifteen interviews, all five phrases were chosen amongst participants, but viewing law enforcement as agents of systematic and institutional brutality was chosen the most frequently.

This is notable because the remaining three phrases involved emotional intensities at the furthest ends of their respective spectrums: contempt, hatred or respect for law enforcement being strong emotional feelings while indifference to the police was a total absence of emotion regarding police. The two that were chosen the most--suspicion of law enforcement and view law enforcement as agents of systematic and institutional brutality--had more to say and spoke most passionately suggesting that the majority of participants had very pensive perceptions of police where those who answered otherwise had less salient points of view.

Thirteen of the fifteen participants viewed law enforcement as agents of systematic and institutional brutality. The remaining two only answered "indifferent to the police": one straight woman and one straight man. All queer people indicated that they believed law enforcement to be agents of systematic and institutional brutality and four of the five straight women and straight men respectively also made this indication.

Nine of the fifteen participants indicated that they were suspicious of law enforcement. Queer Black people led this choice with 4 out 5 indicating suspicion. Not only could this be attributed to the Black community's long and negative history with the police but, it can also be attributed to the LGBT+ community's long and negative history with police particularly where Black queer folks and especially where Black trans women are concerned. Two out of five straight Black women chose this option and three out of five straight Black men chose this option. This difference could possibly speak to Black men's higher likelihood of experiencing police brutality.

Five people total indicated having contempt, hatred or in one respondent's case "disdain" for police. Three of these people were queer, two being trans masculine and one being Amena, a bisexual woman. The other two were men including one man who chose every option. The other man was Ian, a larger statured dark-skinned Black man who had experienced what he perceived as racial profiling numerous times in his life.

Four people total indicated indifference to the police. Two people indicated having respect for police, a very low number out of fifteen. Both could be attributed to the same reason that nine people total indicated being suspicious of the police: a lack of trust due to witnessing and/or experiencing police brutality as a marginalized person in marginalized community/ communities.

In sum, while participants found true value in each of the statements, they tended to agree more with the idea that law enforcement are agents of systematic and institutional brutality and that they were suspicious of law enforcement. The above question was informative as participants spoke about their own experiences with police and society where their bodily autonomy was concerned. These feelings of apathy regarding positive change within policing were also reflected in their views concerning the public and highly politicized murders of unarmed Black people by police.

These participants also confirmed Chaney and Robertson's beliefs regarding Black people's feelings about police as they responded similarly to those in the article. The nuance that was added was done so by including gender and sexual orientation as variables alongside the Black identity. Though overwhelmingly participants spoke about their distrust of the police, they did so based on their experiences through unique combinations of marginalized social locations.

Emergent Themes

The participant responses above served to garner participant attitudes toward police while also setting up the open-ended questions. This is because participants' feelings toward police then framed how they viewed the murders of unarmed Black people by police subsequently, usually viewing these murders as unjust. Utilizing Afro-Pessimism and Intersectionality to understand how young Black people navigate their bodily autonomy in relation to a state of pervasive police violence and an anti-Black society, I discovered the following themes: Black youth are dying too, and it's not getting any better causing hopelessness and in turn anger, performing gender while coping with perceived threats, Black women and dehumanized femininity, and Black men's severe lack of bodily autonomy. Through the themes, it is apparent that under the threat of police violence, how young Black people navigate their bodily autonomy varies by sex, gender identity, and sexuality. The first two themes emerged primarily from the questions about how participants felt about police brutality cases. The final three themes emerged from intersectional questions about participants' own experiences with police and society regarding their bodily autonomy

Black Youth Are Dying Too

These interviews took place almost a year after George Floyd's death but most took place before Derek Chauvin was sentenced to twenty-two and a half years for the murder of Floyd. As such the first two themes are responses to the following questions: "How old are you now? Looking back on the series of killings of African Americans by the police and others, how does that make you feel now?" During the interviews, Derek Chauvin's trial repeatedly came up. One indicator participants gave for the lack of bodily autonomy in their lives was that Black people even younger than them were being killed by the police *still*. In fact the stories of Black death, including those of youth, reaffirm their own experiences in which they encounter the police and suddenly don't feel free to just be themselves in front of the police. During the time period of Chauvin's trial participants juxtaposed the moment with the fact that Black children younger than them were being murdered at the hands of police. This, in their view, was evidence that no real structural change was taking place. For them, Black youth being murdered at the hands of police was what the tragic event of Sandy Hooks, where very young children of elementary participants spoke about not believing the trial would make a societal difference because during the trial unarmed Black people continued to be murdered by police, such as Daunte Wright, who was killed ten miles away from where Chauvin's trial took place. Wright was killed "accidentally" because Officer Kimberly Potter mistook her gun for her taser. Potter's trial was set for December 6th 2021. Daunte Wright was twenty years old. age were murdered, was to gun reform activists which was a sobering look at reality. This also informed their own negative perceptions of their own bodily autonomy.

Some participants spoke about wanting Chauvin to be charged with life in prison due to the brazen and torturous nature of Floyd's death. Other One participant, Lamonte explained his feelings of hopelessness concerning Chauvin's trial as follows,

> It's almost like they're telling us how powerless we are. That's depressing. Even with Derek Chauvin, it doesn't matter if he gets-- Obviously, it matters to George Floyd's family and all of that, but on a structural level, it doesn't matter if he gets convicted because the system is the same either way. It's just going to be either the system going the way it always does if he gets convicted, or just a sacrificial lamb.

During both interviews, whenever we discussed Chauvin's trial or guilty verdict it was being discussed in juxtaposition to another Black person's death at the hands of police, whose name was Ma'Khia Bryant. She was sixteen years old when she called police to her residence because she was being "jumped" or assaulted by multiple people at once. She was subsequently shot in the chest multiple times by a police officer while she brandished a knife during the altercation.

Neither female participant disagreed with the idea that police should have intervened in the altercation, as that was also Bryant's reason for calling them to the scene. What was disputed, however, was the method of intervention and it being deadly. Regarding this, Aliyah said,

I finally went back and realize it's like, "I need to go ahead and read it and watch the video and starting to feel what I've been trying not to feel." I watched the video. I was reading the comments and there're just like, "Yes. Oh, she shouldn't have been fighting and stuff." I'm like, "She had a knife." He had a gun and he fired like four times, and that's unnecessary. It's insane that this is happening. Y'all are saying this. You're just in your YouTube commenters, but you're justifying this during Chauvin's trial, or maybe immediately after Chauvin's trial at that point.

Participants repeated time and time again that Black children are still children even though they seem to be handled like violent adults within the justice system. They reasoned that this adultification of Black children was due to racism and existing stereotypes about Black people. Aliyah also spoke about what Ma'Khia Bryant's death meant to her in comparison to non-Black people and white people specifically. She implied that it is easy to justify the death of someone who does not look like you, but what's harder is hearing about the death of someone who both looks like you and could have been your younger sister. Aliyah echoed these sentiments while reprocessing the murder of Ma'Khia Bryant,

The thing for me that also hurts in my seeing moments of police brutality is that there's building blocks to all of it. What I saw in the video of Ma'Khia, I was just thinking about all the times that Black women, or people are picked on the way like Black women from presumably lower-income areas like speak, and making jokes out of it, and in any way just diminishing Black women and Black girls.

I was just like, "That's probably what went through that man's head. When he fired four shots, he was like, "Oh, this isn't a girl, this isn't a child, this isn't a kid. They're like one of those people from them videos that we all laugh at. They're like one of those people that white TikTokers like to mock and stuff and take the language and dialect, or whatever and copy. That's not a person."

Aliyah furthers her thought by including the intersection of class. She wondered if Bryant's membership in a low-income Black community fueled the officer's We know that through the Crack epidemic and the War on Drugs, low-income Black communities were both demonized in society and heavily surveilled by police. The effects of this era are still felt today.

Jasmine sarcastically noted that murders like Bryant's become more commonplace every day,

> Not us interrupting a shooting with another shooting with another shooting with another shooting with a guilty verdict that was-- We understand he was guilty, but it's not like we didn't have it all on video.

Jasmine's direct and earnest joke that Black people are still being murdered despite "reform" shows just how much Black death has been normalized in our society and within the Black community which largely has become dejected. Aliyah echoed the hopelessness of Jasmine's sentiments by vocalizing her despair regarding how violated Black childhood is from her perspective,

> Then later I was talking to some friends who live in the States and Canada, and they were talking about the responses of police to folks who were protesting in solidarity with the family of Ma'Khia Bryant and other folks who were murdered by police in the same week. I was just like, "You mean to tell me not only is this happening-- Not only was she murdered, but also the police are beating up the kids who are peacefully protesting?" I'm like, "These are babies. These are more babies who are out here trying to fight for their right to live, fight for the right for other with or without the justice system intervening in some way, people to live.

Their anger and lack of catharsis was reflective of the hopelessness that many of the participants felt, which we will discuss next. These participants are calling attention to the intersections between race and age, particularly youth, which should be a time of innocence. Instead of enjoying this time of innocence, Black children, as these participants see it, are stripped of this innocence the moment they become aware of racism and how it impacts them. Young Black girls and boys are seen as inherently capable of violence. According to Afro-Pessimism, this is because Blackness itself has been demonized in our society and even children are not exempt from experiencing this intersection (Wilderson et al. 2017). Upon understanding this intersection they must carry themselves in a non-carefree way typical of people their age or they may find themselves in predicaments similar to Ma"Khia Bryant or Daunte Wright.

And Catharsis Is Hard To Find

Participants expressed various feelings and perceptions in their responses regarding Black youths being killed by police. Some of the common feelings expressed were anger, sadness, fear, inadequacy, helplessness and loneliness. The most common in both participants was anger, thus the next theme is anger due to hopelessness caused by Black youth being murdered in a time period that was supposed to be about racial justice reform and lack of their own bodily autonomy. Some of the participants were able to reach catharsis while others were not. Interestingly, those who spoke most about anger were less likely to express catharsis seemingly due to viewing current events as ongoing and never ending. This is how living within a anti-Black society further impacts Black people's everyday lives by adding another stressor to their lives which they have to cope with. Those who were able to reach catharsis regarding their anger did so by honing in on the agency they had in shared community and activism. Queer Black participants were slightly more likely to be the angriest due to their coincidental above-average involvement and attentiveness towards the political landscape. This theme of anger due to hopelessness and the search for catharsis in agency is particularly notable due to the fact that not everyone is able to reach this catharsis.

This experience of hopelessness due to Black people being harmed at the hands of police and this issue seemingly not getting better also caused anger that for some did not reach catharsis. This anger was also attributed to how this norm manifested in their own lives where they often did not feel that they could go out into the world or interact with police without making concessions to their autonomy because of they are Black people.

Drew and Lamonte, who were both trans masculine individuals, seemed to be the most angry out of the group, followed by Ian who was the only straight Black man of the participants who was both dark skinned *and* of a larger stature. Aliyah also expressed a notable amount of anger as a community organizer who had, had her safety compromised by her university due to her involvement in its political landscape.

Lamonte reflected on his complicated feelings towards police by sharing an experience he had,

> It's just- I don't like them and they make me nervous. I remember I was at a convenience store once. I was standing next to this cop. I was on edge because there was a cop. I was just minding my own business. We were in line. He looked at me. He asked me to see my tattoo. I have a tattoo on my arm. I was wearing short sleeves, so it was covered half by my shirt. It's a solidarity forever tattoo. It's an old union song and slogan. He asked to see and he was just like, "That's cool, man." I was just like, "Do you understand what this is, sir?" [laughs]. I don't know. That was funny. I laughed about that when I left. That goes to the whole thing of-- I'm sure he was a nice person when he took off his uniform, but don't talk to me if you're a cop please because you're not always nice when you're a cop.

Drew's point of view on police brutality reform and the anger caused by it was very representative of the majority who expressed anger. Asserting that reform is not enough, Drew said,

> It makes me mad with the system and everybody who acts like it's okay, and we just need to reform. I feel a lot of anger around that and fearful. For me and my family, other people I care about that are Black are so also fearful. Then each time-, even though after Trayvon Martin, I have no hope. Also because even though   I am against prisons, I do not think it will fix police brutality by sending an officer or anybody to jail, I don't think it will. It's just something about knowing that most people in the system believe that that's the highest form of like, "Okay, we did the right thing," but yet they continue not to do that.

Here Drew's, and also her counterparts', anger is due to a perceived callousness and lack of empathy on the part of mostly white authorities and politicians. This perceived callousness is not just about police brutality reform but also for the events of Black death themselves. Multiple participants noted that Black people, and even Black children, do not receive empathy nor the benefit of the doubt surrounding the events of their murder. Aliyah spoke about her anger concerning the murder of Ma'Khia Bryant, who was just sixteen years old at the time, while also expressing grief,

> I think every, every time someone's killed by police, it hurts me in a different way where I'm thinking like Ma'Khia Bryant, is who I've been thinking about, just because she was murdered in the middle of, or during Chauvin's trial. The trial for Chauvin was happening, and after, other young folks were murdered by police. It's just like we had a whole summer of reckonings......

Above, Aliyah furthers Jasmine's previous point that Black people continue to be killed despite protests and reforms. She also shares how incidents of police brutality and their aftermath can be very taxing for herself and other Black people. Despite these collective Black realities, participants did find comfort and catharsis in the unanimity of the Black community and its intra-communally shared feelings around police brutality. They also found agency in participating in activism for their community. Though many of them expressed that they did not have the ability to self-govern their own persons in everyday life, they could control their actions around advocating for their communities which gave them some hope and ability for catharsis. Amena expressed that what brought her comfort was raising awareness concerning Black people's civil rights as a way to protect her community,

> I definitely am an advocate. Definitely voice my opinion all the time. It makes me feel better about the role I play. I just feel not even for like, approval. I just feel like umm being there supporting people and being a part of that movement just makes me feel like I'm protecting my people. I'm putting this information out there. I'm making everybody aware. I just feel like I'm doing something versus just sitting back and being hopeless and scared all the time. and whatnot.

Hakeem expressed gratitude for the interview affording him the rare chance to discuss what Black people go through in dealing with racism which also showed catharsis through communing with his peers,

> I mean, this is awesome. I'm glad you're doing this study. I really like talking about this. So like, I feel like better honestly, like I, I feel like maybe I need more outlets to talk about stuff like this. I go to the Counseling Center. But a lot of the times I find that I'm talking about, like, philosophical dilemmas I'm having or whatever, but we don't really talk about just what it feels like to be Black. Like, a lot of times, I feel like I have to suppress this type of conversation. Just because I'm around mostly white people and they- a lot of them just don't understand. Right?

This need to suppress what it is like to be Black is consistent with both institutional racism and the ideology of White Supremacy. This is due to white people, and their collective feelings, being the default in our western society. This is also due to institutional racism and the devaluation of both Black people themselves as well as their thoughts, ideas, and opinions. Both also contribute to the anger Black people feel around police brutality as well as Black people's assumed guilt in these instances of brutality. Despite this, Black people continue to find strength in both fighting for their community and communing within it, which potentially offers them agency and catharsis.

One latent function of the Black Lives Matter movement on Black people has been increased pride in their Blackness due to the agency found in being in community with each other. Several of my participants remarked on the pride they felt in being Black when thinking about the Black community and its allies coming together to demand racial equality and to put an end to police brutality. Here, focusing on how community activism can make positive impacts help to soothe some anger regarding the lack of bodily autonomy Black people have when in the world, especially during police interactions.

Jasmine spoke about her feelings toward Black Lives Matter and Black people's right to exist freely,

> It made me proud that there's one large statement for this situation. I felt before I knew, or I guess it was more mainstream to be about Black Lives Matter, there wasn't a tagline for us to just say, "this is what we're expecting from America, and this is the truth." I feel I was proud to be black. I was proud to have that hashtag, to have that tag everywhere.

Despite Jasmine's previous sense of hopelessness she shared that she is still very proud to be Black, indicating that her negative experiences she has had as a result of being Black has not impacted her own perceptions of herself. Ian also shared this sentiment. Ian spoke about the

confidence in his Blackness that the Black Lives Matter movement has given him,

> So, I think it kind of goes back to the, to the movement, you said, from back in the
> day that my Black is beautiful. That is exactly how I feel. That's exactly how I
> feel. I mean, like I said, the whole world needs to know that I'm Black. And I'm
> okay with it. And everybody else needs to be okay with it.... And for years, so you
> know, I didn't dress how I wanted didn't act how I wanted, kept my hair cut low.
> And at this point, man, we can do what we want. And if anybody has a problem,
> then it is what it is. We got a problem.

Here Ian spoke of how racist experiences he had in his life did impact his own perceptions

of his Blackness through his lack of bodily autonomy due to feeling limited to what he could

wear or how he styled his hair. It was only after he took back his bodily autonomy that he

became more confident in his Blackness. Hakeem shared this same sentiment of finding

confidence in his Blackness through the Black Lives Matter Movement,

> I would say the Black Lives Matter movement made me feel Honestly, it gave me
> a lot of strength, like a lot of baseline level of strength that I felt like I didn't have
> before. Before I learned about like, Black Lives Matter. And before I started,
> really, when I came to college was when I started learning, like more heavily
> about race, the Black Lives Matter movement gave me that initial foundation to
> start looking at myself as not inferior or, or superior to any other race, it just gave
> me this baseline level to start saying, This is who I am, I have literally no control
> over my skin color. So anybody that looks down on me, I feel is actually inferior
> because they are giving into some, some sort of tradition or
> some sort of need to justify oppression.

These sentiments are reminiscent of both the My Black Is Beautiful campaign and the

earlier era of "Say It Loud - I'm Black and I'm Proud" soundtracked by the James Brown's song

of the same name. Like the Black Lives Matter movement, both periods of Black pride were

accompanied by periods of struggle for Black Americans. The My Black Is Beautiful campaign of 2006 came after the crack epidemic of the nineties which unfairly targeted Black Americans, a sentiment that is widely accepted today (Swaminathan et al.. 2020; Koontz and Nguyen 2020). The Say It Loud – I'm Black and I'm Proud era took place during the Civil Rights era and iconic events such as Dr. Martin Luther King Jr.'s I Have A Dream speech, which took place five years before the debut of Brown's song, as well as the Black Power movement which took place in the 1960s and the 1970s (Andrew 2013; Fouché 2006; Joseph 2009). These time periods reflect the resiliency of Black Americans through enduring anti-Black society which has plagued them since their arrival in the West as enslaved peoples.

This intra-communal resiliency of identity is one that has always persevered. The Black and Proud/ Black Power movement, The My Black Is Beautiful campaign, and the Black Lives Matter movement are different eras in our American history but within the community that time is reflected as a generational and intentional passing down of values and identity. In activism for the Black community this passed-down identity becomes agency. These had to be passed down because without doing so the institutional racism of our Western society would have informed the Black community of who they were and are instead of the community defining itself.

The murders of George Floyd, Tony McDade, and Breonna Taylor, among many other Black people, were brought to the forefront of our nation's collective consciousness by the civil unrest of the summer of 2020, which focused our collective consciousness on police violence. The ensuing protests brought this to light among many other non-Black people as Black people themselves have always been aware of this dehumanization since their arrival in America (Wilderson et al. 2017). These deaths were unjustified and preventable, but they are only a small part of the slew of state-sanctioned police brutality practices deployed against Black people. Although Black women are not killed by police at nearly the same rate as Black men, once we understand the complete meaning of police violence, we can see how Black women also face disproportionately high rates of police violence, particularly when it comes to sexual assault and abuse just as their queer counterparts experience a non-monolithic violence themselves due to their Blackness.

Interacting with Society and Police without Bodily Autonomy

The last three themes reflect the less focused on intersectional aspects of police violence and Black people's lack of bodily autonomy in our society. Questions such as the following lent themselves to uncovering how the participants' other marginalized social locations impacted their raced experiences of police brutality and a lack of bodily autonomy in society. These questions included: "Have you ever felt profiled? By whom? For what reason- race, gender, or sexuality?" "Has there ever been a time you felt discriminated against by anyone because of two or more of your identities together pertaining to race, gender, and/or sexual orientation?" "Have you ever been harassed or assaulted by the police? In what way?" "How does the threat of police brutality change your daily routine if at all?" "Are there things you fear doing because of fear of personal/ professional safety?" "Do you feel you have to act differently in the presence of the police? Why or why not?"

Black Women and Dehumanized Femininity

Black women in America must contend with stereotypes about them that define them as less feminine and more aggressive in their everyday lives. Amena and Aliyah both spoke about how there was nothing they could do as Black women to lessen the likelihood of police harassment or brutality due to this issue. Amena was a dark-skinned bisexual Black woman of a relatively larger stature and Aliyah was a brown skinned Black woman of a larger stature. Their experiences with colorism and stereotyping Black women was very different from my own experiences. In contrast, as a petite, brown skinned Black woman I found that there was more that I could personally do to dissuade police harassment and brutality, including code switching, which many Black people do in these instances, which for me included "turning up my femininity." This entails things like making my voice higher, holding my body a certain way so that I take up less space, and wearing feminine clothing such as ensuring that my winter coat is a fluffy pink jacket. Both of these women expressed that this was not an option for them when I told them about my experiences during our conversations. Aliyah explicitly indicated that this was because of her size. She explained this through the following,

> I feel like, I don't know if [femininity is] an option for me and maybe there's a point where maybe earlier I would have been like, "Maybe it's an option." I don't know. I've been recognizing, I'm a larger person. I'm 5'6." That makes me a little [self-]conscious.

Amena cited the attitude of police reason why femininity and changing her appearance does not aide her in intercepting any possibility of experiencing police brutality,

> I don't think they really care too much about how you present yourself. Because if they just have hatred, like, they don't really care, but I do, I will say it was a time where I would like wear my ECU shirt everywhere I would go because I'll be thinking like, maybe if they see that I'm a hard working college student, they're less likely to harass me or target me or whatnot. But at this point, I'm just kind of, like, I don't really see any decency and humanity from them. I don't really think they care. They pulled over and pepper sprayed a guy that was in the army, or not sure if it was the army, but so it's like, they don't care. They don't even care if you're in the police force with them. They don't care if you're law enforcement yourself like, I don't know.

As previously discussed, this issue of gender presentation in front of the police is an intersectional one that Black queer people, have to also consider. This demonstrates how Black women's issue of gender presentation in front of the police is also an intersectional matter because it exists because they are both Black and women.

Afro-Pessimism asserts that "femininity loses its sacredness in slavery…. To that extent, the captive female body locates precisely a moment of converging political and social vectors that mark the flesh as a prime commodity of exchange" (Spillers 2017:112). Today, this loss of access to femininity is something that Black women are constantly made aware of. Societally, femininity comes with a certain paternalization that is condescending but also serves as a badge of innocence. Conversely, Black women are societally assumed not to be innocent. When in interactions with the police, because Black women do not possess access to societal femininity and in turn, innocence, police are more comfortable subjecting them to violence. Police do so because Black women are Black but are aided by the social circumstances around being both Black and women. Amena also shared an incident in which police assumed she was a sex worker after pulling herself and her uncle over who had just picked her up from the hospital. Despite sharing this, and also still wearing her hospital bracelet, the police officers involved did not change their implicative demeanor,

> They pulled us over and they were asking us questions. And they were like, why are you in the car with him? I'm like, this is my uncle I just came from the hospital. He's picking me up. And they were like, well, if that's your uncle- like, they like kind of were questioning the legitimacy of our relationship. And it kind of pissed me off, because it's like, you're trying to imply that I have sexual relations with this man. This man is my uncle, and whatnot. And yall don't even have a valid reason. Then they asked us to step out the car so they can check the car for any illegal substances and weapons and whatnot.

And then by that time, two other police cars had pulled up. And it was like a woman and a younger cop. And she was insistent on like, patting me down for no reason. And the guy was like, we already checked her ID there's no reason he was like, she was like you sure? Like I think we should pat her down, I'm like, nobody's going to touch me. Like, don't put your hands on me. I don't consent to being pat down. There's no reason for you to pat me down. I just came from the hospital, clearly there's a brace on my arm. It just made me angry.

Amena's above experience personifies the way in which Black women do not receive assumed innocence in the way that their white peers do. This is furthered by the fact that Amena is a dark skinned Black woman because her darker skin resulted in her gendered innocence being seen as non-existent as the involved police officers immediately were under the impression that she was a sex worker despite other evidence being available such as her hospital bracelet which corroborated her story.

Amena and Aliyah exemplify what Black women's lived experiences can look like when they do not have access to femininity and in turn the presumed innocence that comes with femininity (Davis 2018). This is not a monolithic issue because some Black women have more access to femininity if they have features or attributes that appeal to white beauty standards such as lighter skin, smaller facial features, straight hair, or being an expert in code switching. (Davis 2018).

Black women societally do not have access to femininity and in turn innocence but for dark–skinned Black women they are seen as even less innocent due to colorism, acting as almost a second dose of the angry Black woman stereotype (Davis 2018). Layla nervously made this connection by expressing her frustrations regarding femininity as a dark-skinned Black woman,

> I'm darker skinned as well. It was just like, …. "Am I acting feminine?" It's just that Intersectionality just sometimes starts to get very, very annoying. Then it's like I have to question myself. Again, that's me having to share "me" with people

who will not understand me most of the time or will most likely not really care for me.

Tamara furthered the idea of colorism as being a second dose of the angry Black woman stereotype by explaining,

> Going back to the colorism thing, I don't want to like end the interview without saying something about it. Because I do feel like I do experience that more. And I think, for me it's definitely that being a darker female, getting that she has an attitude vibe. And that's something that I have to deal with. Even at work, I feel like I still kind of experience it a little, a little bit. Despite the company being diverse. There's still some of the people that I work with may- if I don't say it a certain way, or let them know, I don't have an attitude or whatever. It might be taken differently. But yeah.

These experiences further the issue of Black women not having societal access to femininity and innocence because that includes every moment of their lived experiences, as well as interactions with the police. Even if these interactions do not end in brutality, police may similarly mistake them for having attitudes and treat them accordingly due to societal and colorist stereotypes around dark-skinned Black women. Black women's lack of access to societal femininity and the stereotypes about them, particularly dark-skinned Black women, can be attributed to the way in which they systematically experience dehumanization, racism, and colorism.

Layla shared an exemplary experience of hers in which she was stereotyped while also being dark-skinned young girl,

When I was younger, I had to be in elementary school. I'm going to try to say around between the ages of seven and nine, me and my group of friends hanging at the mall as young people do. I'm going to say a little bit older. I'm going to say we were probably a little bit older. Even then, it was still just hanging out, our parents are just hanging out as well. We just went into Claire's specifically and we were just told that we need to split up because we looked suspicious.

Even as young girls Black women do not have the privilege of being perceived as innocent. Black girls have no bodily autonomy in just being young girls because instead they must learn the pitfalls of racism early in age in order to circumvent stereotypes about Black criminality. Thusly, Black girls do not experience the fullness of joy in Black girlhood as their white peers are able to. Instead they are thrust into womanhood by having to contend with what their skin color means in their society at an early age. They have no option of opting out of this.

Black Men and a Severe Lack of Bodily Autonomy

In the United States Black men must contend with aggressive stereotypes about their masculinity. The straight Black men that I interviewed typically were the most likely to experience repeated harassment by police, four of the five, as well as the most likely to change their behavior for an extended period of time in front of the police due to this issue. This theme regarding Black masculinity is unsurprising in the wake of the idea that Black femininity is dehumanized due to Black people's societal label as deviant. Kahlil spoke about his encounters with police by highlighting an idea and way of existing around police he called "walking with a purpose" which he was taught by his uncle, saying,

And I guess it's because he grew up in that time where it was a lot of oppression that he went through he's like all right when you're walking somewhere walk with a purpose, so like, walk with your head up like, you're going somewhere like you have somewhere to be. So yeah, whenever I'm around, and I know there's cops, like, on the street and stuff I turn from like, if I'm just chilling, I'm just enjoying my day walking, I start walking more so with a purpose to make it seem like, I'm not just- I don't even know what the word would be loitering? I don't know. Um, so there's no reason for them to stop me and ask questions or anything like that.

Kahlil went on to talk about how he had gotten so used to "walking with a purpose" that it felt natural, but it did impede on his feelings of bodily autonomy or ability to self-govern because he should not have to feel like he has to do these things to survive. He then went on to further expound upon what walking with a purpose is, including taking off a hoodie, implying that someone wearing a hoodie could not be seen as someone who would have contributions to make as a participating member of society. This was from the viewpoint of his lived experience as a young dark--skinned Black man. In the following quote he explains what walking with a purpose entails,

I think like you mentioned with the more high-pitched voice or anything like that you almost turn into, like, when you're on a phone call for an interview, or when you're stopping at the drive thru, like that, that voice comes on. And then like I said earlier just walking with a purpose. Umm, act like I'm- I have somewhere to be type thing. Or even like with hoodies, sometimes, like taking my hoodie off or umm, yeah yeah, stuff like that.

It is important to note that Black men only experience male privilege within the Black community. When they are in white society, their Black masculinity is actually a hinderance specifically because they are also Black. This violent and normalized racism specific to Black men like Khalil, not being able to even walk down the street without considering the implications of doing so serves as the source of the reason Black men are deprived of the ability to control their bodies and identities in police interactions but also in the general public sphere. Prejudicially, Black manhood is seen as inherently deviant.

This idea of walking with a purpose resonated with other Black men that I interviewed to varying degrees. Ian, for example, identified with the idea of trying to avoid police by walking with a purpose but because he was both dark skinned and of a larger stature this was less available to him and men who look like him. Speaking on his feelings toward police Ian said,

> They [law enforcement] make scenarios worse, and people are actually afraid to call them. Because they don't want to, they don't want anything to happen to them. So it's like, who do you call then if you can't call whoever's supposed to serve and protect you? You know what I mean? So definitely some disdain. And yes, I do believe they do enforce systematic oppression. There's so many instances where they lock up Black men for essentially nothing or whatever they have found, or maybe even planted.

Like Khalil, Ian spoke about being deprived of his ability to control his body and identity due to systemic racism but also in his case due to colorism and his size which is exemplified in his experience of an instant in which campus police were called during a time in which he was a new student discovering his campus,

> I went in, and I walked past a professor's room and the door was wide open. And I just, I just knock knock knocked. And I was like, excuse me, what exactly is this building? I noticed there's a bunch of fashion stuff. And then she basically goes, can you step out, please. So I step out, she wants to see my student ID, I did not want to show her. But if I didn't show her, I knew she would probably call campus PD. So I showed her my student ID, and she told me what the building was. So I think I ended up going down to the lobby, and I just sat down for a little bit on my phone, just because I mean, it was a nice building. And I see campus PD walked by me. And I knew that they were going to turn back around and talk to me. And they did turn back around and talked to me. And she was basically like, oh, everything's fine. I think you just scared the lady or

something like that. But I mean, I don't really know how I scared her when the door was wide open. And she saw me and I knocked on the door.

Here we see what it is like to live at the multiple intersections of the non-monolithic Black male experience and colorism attributed to having darker skin, both of which have been labeled deviant in our society.

Hakeem spoke about this idea of walking with a purpose saying that for him it also included ideas around masculinity,

> Because I think it's like also like kind of living up to manhood or whatever. Like showing that you're, you're not weak, per se. And just also showing that like you, like you said, like walking with purpose that you're actually doing something. And like even going back to what we were saying about Publix and Harris Teeter, when I'm in those stores, I do feel a lot more comfortable when I actually have a cart in front of me or when I have like, like bags in my hand or something like that. Just because if I look like I'm doing something already, then it's like, well, you're not gonna discriminate against me, because you can obviously see I'm doing the same thing you're doing. But if I'm just in there with nothing, I just feel like they're assuming I'm about to steal something or something like that.

Isaiah spoke about his agency related to an interaction with the police by describing the following incident, "I was wearing my durag at the time and I had on a chain. Me trying to just automatically alleviate the situation to not be as aggressive or threatening, I took the durag off and I tucked the chain into my shirt." When asked if he felt like he had bodily autonomy or the ability to self-govern in that instance he said,

> I think I did because I consciously did that on purpose. I intentionally took it off. I think the reasoning behind it might not be good because it's like that's part of my culture. It's literally just for a hairstyle. That's what durags are for, but we're so culturally different and apart that, that's just a sign of certain activities to certain

people. They don't understand because we don't share certain cultural things. I was like, I'm just going to be neutral and just not have anything that would make them want to discriminate or have any views towards me.

When Isaiah spoke about durags being "a sign of certain activities to certain people" he is still referencing the Black social death inherent to Black people and Black culture in Western society, which sees them as inherently deviant, despite asserting that he had bodily autonomy. Viewed through the lens of Afro-Pessimism, this begs the question: Can Black people have the ability to self-govern when the racism of their society is like an ocean, all around them? Also, if a Black person is a fish in this ocean of racism, do they then always know they are wet? Could they get used to being wet or entrenched in systematically racist experiences, just as Kahlil got used to walking with a purpose?

When asked if he felt that he had to remove his durag and tuck his chain he said, "I don't think I had to do it, but I guess my way of thinking was, I just want this process to be as smooth as possible and be on my way. I don't want anything to happen right now." He also explained that he was accompanied by a woman and because of this he was most worried about her safety. Therefore, his idea of masculinity may have impacted his decisions as was the case for Kahlil who viewed "walking with a purpose" as just part of Black male life.

Malik, a brown-skinned Black man of a larger stature who has had both positive and negative interactions with police said this when speaking about them,

I feel all of it. All mixes of those emotions because I hate them, I respect them, I feel indifferent towards them. Out in public, I try to ignore them. I do think they work in a systematic way to oppress people… I'm suspicious that they would do something to make it go their way. I feel all those feelings towards police officers.

Malik's viewpoint of the police was one that all of the other Black participants would agree with based on their own interviews making it a great example of Black men's encounters with police. As a result, some of the Black men I interviewed who had been harassed or assaulted by the police also were more likely to express contempt for police in addition to other emotions such as suspicion of the police and viewing them as agents of systematic oppression during closed-ended questions. Much of their strong and unwavering feelings about police were in response to their own lack of bodily autonomy and fear of persecution by the police and those who might levy law enforcement against them.

The Black Queer Community and Performing Gender

Three of the five LGBT+ identified folks I interviewed expressed that in order to preemptively deter themselves from experiencing police brutality they would change their gender expression in the presence of police officers. For two of these participants, both trans masculine individuals, this caused what they described as gender dysphoria which is when people assume one's gender to be a gender contrary to their actual gender identity. Notably, for queer Black people, a lack of bodily autonomy and agency not only means the inability to self-govern because our society is insidiously anti-Black but it also means fear of LGBT discrimination in our heteronormative society for some folks.

Lamonte spoke about the gender dysphoria he experiences when dealing with police encounters because he is seen as a "twink," which is defined as being a feminine man, even though he doesn't consider himself to be feminine. He also said that this helps him during police encounters because he is viewed as non-threatening saying,

But also though I do have a privilege in terms of passing. As a trans person, I pass I'd say pretty well. I'm very twinkish, but I pass very well in the context of being twinkish, I guess. I probably am masculine presenting rather than feminine presenting. It's pretty well established that there's a particularly harsh and negative spotlight on transwomen, Black trans women specifically.

Here Lamonte expresses the dissonance between his lived experience and being faced with what heteronormative society assigns him to be. It is because he is a trans masculine person that he is seen as a twink when by police, which translates to being non-threatening because femininity is societally stereotyped this way. The harm to Lamonte here is done intersectionally because not only do his interactions with police prevent him from owning himself and his identity through gender dysphoria but he felt he must endure these encounters without reclaiming his identity. This was due to the intersectional ways in which he experienced institutional racism, which causes an inability to self-govern, he could experience as a Black person encountering police.

Drew spoke about how the threat of police brutality affected their agency and contributed to gender dysphoria, especially because they are still figuring their gender out as a young person. Drew said that they preferred to dress more masculine but they did not feel safe doing so because they noticed that when they did the police were more likely to notice them and watch them intently. They also added,

If I'm dressed more masculine, then I'm going to be perceived as a Black man and a threat. If I'm dressed more feminine, which that happens sometimes, then I'm going to be perceived as a Black woman, someone who they could do whatever to. It may not be a threat, but they can still treat me in whatever way, and what can I do about it?

This quote exemplified their feelings about the police being agents of systematic and institutional brutality because they did not believe there is any instance where Black people can escape being seen as deviant regardless of gender, in spite of Black femininity and especially in the presence of Black masculinity. It also points to how femininity does not inherently prevent all Black women from experiencing police brutality due to the way in which institutional racism is normalized in our society. Here Drew expresses the dissonance between their lived experience and being faced with white heteronormative society forcing them to choose between non-guaranteed safety through donning a feminine gender expression, and thus gender dysphoria, and expected suspicion and aggression from police if donning a gender-confirming masculine expression of themself. It is because they are a Black trans masculine person that they are forced to make this choice when encountering police. The harm to Drew here is done Intersectionally because not only do their interactions with police prevent them from owning themself and their identity due to gender dysphoria but they felt they must endure these encounters without reclaiming their identity due to the societally normalized racism they believe they would experience as a Black masculine person encountering police based on their former experiences with police.

These parallels between masculine genderqueer folks and being perceived as having a feminine gender expression coincidentally highlight the demeaning way in which society thinks of femininity. However, there are several intersectionalities to consider. We have already discussed the Intersectionality of femininity regarding women, trans masculine folks, and/or gender queer folks, but race is also a point of Intersectionality to consider, regarding who has access to femininity.

Andre spoke about playing up their femininity in the presence of the police so as not to be seen as a threat. They viewed this as an essential part of their survival but that it had also become a regular part of their life because they are a dark-skinned Black man of a larger stature. They described their experiences in the following way,

I basically disguise myself if that makes sense. Especially when I'm wearing more manly type of things. When I'm wearing feminine clothes, then that's just like, it's kind of an obvious thing. Like if I'm wearing a sweatsuit because Trayvon Martin was wearing a sweatsuit and just jeans, baggy jeans, and stuff like that, I always try to present myself as more feminine in my gay aspect than I usually am, just to disguise myself, which is crazy.

Like Lamonte, Andre experiences their perceived femininity as helping them to appear misogynistically non-threatening due to societal norms. Unlike Lamonte, Andre does this intentionally by performing their femininity when in the presence of police. Their reason for doing so was because their experience of moving through the world as a LGBT+ dark-skinned Black man has informed the reality of many obstacles in their life due to these marginalizations, which prevent them from doing so freely and self-governed. This is personified when Andre spoke about an experience they had being followed around in a store and they didn't know if it was due to their being LGBT+, Black, dark-skinned, larger statured or a combination of these social locations,

If you got a problem with Black people-" I was just like, "Just have a problem with Black people and just be straight up." She said, "What, I do not have a problem with Black people. Where did you get that from?" I was like, "Because you've been following me around in the store, man. You've been following me. There's no other thing to get from that. I'm a Black-- Do you have a problem with gay people?" She said, "No." She immediately said no. I'm like, "Oh, so you don't have a problem with gay people. Now I know it is a Black thing because you just got sideways defensive about it being a Black thing. Why didn't you get sideways defensive about it being the gay thing?" She just looked at me like I was stupid. She looked confused and dumbfounded. I was like, "Thank you. Have a good day, babe." I walked out of the store.

I interviewed four people whose gender identities are considered non-normative, three being trans and one being non-binary. Of these four genderqueer people, Lamonte, Drew, and

Andre shared that they felt that they had to perform heteronormative gender for police, especially because they were also Black. This highlights that this conversation about Black People and the ability to self-govern as it pertains to police brutality is an intersectional one as well as one that is systematic, being born of systems entrenched in normalized racism. Since we know that normalized, institutional racism exists and permeates our age-old and generationally passed down systems then we can acknowledge its other name: White Supremacy. It is an intersectional one because Black queer folks have to consider their multiple oppressions while endeavoring through life because they do so being both Black and queer at the same time, always. These Black queer identified detrimental experiences are indicators that transphobia, racism and White Supremacy are still prevalent in our modern society.

Bodily Autonomy Across Black Intersections

In sum, I found that for Black women respondents, their lack of bodily autonomy in interactions with the police came from societal stereotypes about them having attitudes and being less feminine. Dark-skinned Black women in particular had to contend with how these stereotypes translated to the lack of innocence that comes with femininity in their lives including in interactions with the police. This limited their bodily autonomy to trying not to be perceived in accordance with these stereotypes during these interactions for fear of police retaliation. Black men suffered the most from a lack of bodily autonomy in interactions with police. During the course of the interviews, a phenomenon that came to be referred to as "walking with a purpose" was an experience many of the Black male respondents identified with. Walking with a purpose included Black men going from casually walking in the public sphere to walking as if they had somewhere to be when in the presence of police. It also included not wearing hoodies and other clothing commonly worn by Black people. These men learned how to do so at very young ages from older Black men in their lives. They also expressed that they had to do this specifically because they were both Black and men due to Black masculinity being stereotyped as deviant in society. In a sense, during these interactions with police Black men were not self-governing their bodies and instead were being governed by institutionalized anti-Blackness. For many of the men, this even became a part of their identities as they grew older while interacting with police over the years. For Black trans masculine respondents, the lack of bodily autonomy they experienced in interactions with the police was the gender dysphoria they experienced when police misgendered them and they didn't feel allowed to correct them. Some of these respondents indicated that they also were afraid of police gendering them as masculine because of how the police interact with Black men. They also noted that safety for Black women was also not guaranteed due to their seeming disposability in society. In the next section I discuss these findings in light of the extant literature.

Chapter 5: DISCUSSION

In this study I interviewed fifteen young Black people to interrogate how they experienced their bodily autonomy within the context of pervasive police violence. My research questions were: "Do young Black people feel they have bodily autonomy in interactions with the police under the threat of police brutality and what can this reveal about their everyday lives? How does this experience vary by gender, gender identity and/or sexuality?"

From the interviews, several themes emerged. These themes reflected intersectional societal issues pertaining to Black people's constrained bodily autonomy under pervasive police violence. It is important to note that the generalizability of this study can be argued against due to its sample size. However, it can also be argued that such a perspective is more reflective of the quantitative approach rather than the qualitative approach that this study follows which is also culturally based (Lindsay-Dennis 2015).

Police Brutality from the Black Point of View and Mental Health

What became abundantly clear through interviewing my young, Black participants was the toll the experience and threat of police brutality had on their psyche. The dismay and hopelessness in which they spoke about public cases of police brutality and their own brushes with police harassment was deeply embedded into them as a latent function of being Black. This is because these feelings were crucial for their survival. Their apathy regarding Black people's experiences of society allowed them the passivity and bandwidth needed to survive interactions with police and other bureaucratic, carceral institutions such as micro-aggressions in the work place. This bandwidth was founded in the belief that their anti-Black experiences would never be meaningfully improved.

However, what this passivity stole from them was more than just their hope. It went further by stealing even their hope for the idea of hope; casting it in shadows that spoke of naiveite. Without hope many participants, particularly the queer ones, found it hard to find any catharsis or way of dealing with their heavy feelings. While some participants did find comfort, and inklings of hope, in the strength of their communities in activism, for many this too felt to naive in the face of the bureaucracy of their society against their activism. I believe that this restlessness of the spirit speaks most closely to the Black experience which is to suffer and maneuver through everyday life under the weight and insidiousness of anti-Blackness.

Constrained Bodily Autonomy due to Pervasive Police Violence

Black people's bodily autonomy is significantly constrained to the pervasive threat of police violence due to White supremacy and Anti-Blackness. From an Afro-Pessimist perspective, Black people in the United States lost their humanity and bodily autonomy with the inception of Americanized slavery which cast them as objects and not people (Patterson 1985; Wilderson et al... 2017). From this origin, Blackness is pathologized, Black people are perceived as inherently suspect, deviant (Brooms and Clark 2020; Carbado 2017).

As a result, Black people are "1) open to gratuitous violence, as opposed to violence contingent upon some transgression or crime; 2) natally alienated, their ties of birth not recognized and familial structures intentionally broken apart; and 3) generally dishonored, or disgraced before any thought or action is considered" (Wilderson et al. 2017: 8). Young Black people's perceptions of items one and three are evident within the bounds of the present study.

For example, Amena wore college t-shirts on a regular basis as a way to signal to police that she was not a threat. In addition, another example would be Tamara's experience of being stopped by a Black police officer who scolded her about not putting herself in the position to be stopped by the police. This is important and notable because societally we invoke police as people who serve and protect citizens; so why would being stopped by the police be assumed to be a detrimental experience if they are just serving and protecting? The subtext of the conversation did not need to be said aloud because the conversation was between two Black people, Tamara and the Black police officer, who are literally always being governed by this subtext. A third example would be Layla's experience shopping in Claire's as a young teen and being told that her and her friends looked "suspicious" simply because Black childhood has never been given the benefit of the doubt or innocence. If your choices are not freely made of your own accord and instead influenced by outside forces, such as everyday racism, then they lack the "fullness" of complete personhood. This is something Black Americans understand all too well through inherited generational trauma and persecution (Ransby 2018). These are indicators of constrained bodily autonomy.

Overall, participants experience significant constraints in their bodily autonomy due to the pervasiveness of police violence. This means that they have limited agency or capacity to act during interactions with police and survive the contact without violence, potentially deadly violence. Black people are not free to act independently because they must consider how deviant stereotypes about them will impact their ability to move through the world and live (Greene et al. 2021). Yet how young Black people experience, react, and navigate life in the pervasiveness of police violence varies by sex, gender identity, and sexuality.

I found that for Black women respondents, their lack of bodily autonomy in interactions with the police came from societal stereotypes about them having attitudes and being less feminine. Dark-skinned Black women in particular had to contend with how these stereotypes translated to the lack of innocence that comes with femininity in their lives, including in interactions with the police. This limited their bodily autonomy to trying not to be perceived in accordance with these stereotypes during these interactions for fear of police retaliation. The chivalry hypothesis indicates that women who adhere to traditional gender norms are afforded more leniency in our society (Greene et al. 2021). One could argue that white femininity is the epitome of this phenomenon because white women are the default for what women should be in our society. Black women do not fit easily into these traditional gender norms and are not afforded its "chivalry" especially dark-skinned Black women and this includes in police interactions. An example of this would be Amena's story in which she was stopped by police while her uncle was taking her home after she had just been emitted from the hospital. From Amena's perspective, the police officers immediately began to imply that she might have been a sex worker without giving a reason for this assumption. This was in spite of the fact that she was still wearing her hospital bracelet which was concurrent with her recantation of her day to police. Here, Amena's femininity received no chivalry because she did not fit into white traditional gender norms as a dark-skinned Black woman of a larger stature.

Black men suffered substantially from a lack of bodily autonomy in interactions with police. During the course of the interviews, a phenomenon that came to be referred to as "walking with a purpose" was an experience many of the Black male respondents identified with. Walking with a purpose included Black men going from casually walking in the public sphere to walking as if they had somewhere to be when in the presence of police. It also included not wearing hoodies and other clothing commonly worn by Black people. These men learned how to do so at very young ages from older Black men in their lives. They also expressed that they had to do this specifically because they were both Black and men due to Black masculinity being stereotyped as deviant in society. In a sense, during these interactions with police Black men were not self-governing their bodies and instead were being governed by institutionalized anti-Blackness. For many of the men, this even became a part of their identities as they grew older while interacting with police over the years. This required practice of walking with a purpose can be attributed to Black misandry. Black misandry "refers to an exaggerated pathological aversion toward Black men created and reinforced in societal, institutional, and individual ideologies, practices, and behaviors," which exists "to justify and reproduce the subordination and oppression of Black men." The intersecting identities of Black boys and men provide a double burden due to race (e.g., anti-Black racism) and gender (e.g., anti-Black male attitudes or Black misandry) (Brooms and Clark 2020: 128).

For Black trans masculine respondents, the lack of bodily autonomy they experienced in interactions with the police was the gender dysphoria they experienced when police misgendered them and they didn't feel allowed to correct them. Some of these respondents indicated that they also were afraid of police gendering them as masculine because of how the police interact with Black men. They also noted that safety for Black women was also not guaranteed due to their seeming disposability in society. Examples of this include Drew explaining their fear of being read as masculine by police paradoxically existing with her knowledge that to be read as a Black woman, *not* feminine, would be the same as being disposable. While disposability was recognized as a horrible fate, being read as a Black masculine person was a fate that invoked intense fear. Black trans women also know the dangers of being read as masculine if they don't "pass" as cisgendered women in our society because passing can be synonymous with safety due the violent transphobia that they specifically endure. This is further evidenced by their short life expectancy of thirty-five years of age (CDC 2015). The precarity of Black queer existence is worsened by the community-wide exclusion of them in Black Lives Matter conversations, despite the movement being started by queer Black women, and also the LGBT+ rights movement sidelining issues that are specific to Black queer people only.

Black Women and White Beauty Standards in Society

Since the anti-Black racists and White supremacists needed to control Black bodies during American slavery, Blackness itself has been masculinized because femininity cannot be cast as brutish, as enslaved people were cast due to their not being seen as humans but only objects (Patterson 1985; Wilderson et al. 2017). Typically, in American culture and many cultures across the globe womanhood is associated with femininity. Femininity is misogynistically paternalized as weak; this is condescending but it also has a latent function as a badge of innocence. This idyllic femininity is not enjoyed by Black women specifically because they have been historically dehumanized in turn dehumanizing their access to femininity and innocence (Collins 2000). This is particularly true for Black women who are of darker complexions and larger statures including in police interactions and events of brutality (Crutchfield et al. 2018; Wilder 2008).

For Black women today this dehumanization and defeminization is coupled with assumed deviance which can mean a lack of bodily autonomy in police interactions, which are not immune to stereotypes about them (Greene et al. 2021). The Black women I interviewed expressed that they had experienced upsetting interactions with police due to the idea that societally Black women are often-deprived of their femininity. They felt it left them more vulnerable to police brutality than their other cisgender female peers because of their being both Black and women, at all times, always (Davis 2018). This conversation also spoke on how these conversations are also about how police brutality is *systematic* while also being intersectional (Davis 2018).

Heteronormatively, femininity is seen as both weak and non-threatening. This is due to women's historical subjugation in Western society and the idea that societally femininity is defined as being owned by women. The latent function of this oppression is more safety for feminine women and anyone else who presents as feminine, defined by Western beauty standards, in the presence of police, excluding some Black and darker-skinned women and non-binary people who experience societally normed racism intersectionally. This results in Black women being deprived of their bodily autonomy due to the stereotypes about them.

Black women are subject to violence in this way not only because they are not human because of their blackness, but also because they are not seen as feminine, ideal women, because of their race (Collins 2000). In their study of Black women subjected to police raids, Greene and colleagues (2021) found that Black women perceived police to regard them through stereotyped lenses. Thus, as Black women navigate their bodily autonomy with police, they perform gender in ways to make themselves more safe – deploying femininity as a protective shield (Greene et al.. 2021).

Black Men, Vulnerability, and Masculinity Expectations

As we have discussed previously, Black men are particularly vulnerable to police violence due to their intersection of being both Black and men in their anti-Black Western society. This intersection is particularly notable because Black men do not benefit from male privilege *outside of their community* and are actually marginalized by it. Societally, Black people suffer through negative stereotypes that frame them to be untrustworthy. Combine this with the idea that straight Black men typically do not have access to femininity and it's no surprise that they are often wrongfully harassed by the police. The threat of this wrongful harassment means that Black men must be governed by their very real fears of police brutality.

Also, with this unique intersection that Black men occupy comes heightened masculinity expectations that their white counterparts experience to a lesser degree. Any perceived femininity in straight Black men is seen as emasculating. This is due to the institutionally racist history of western society and the racist emasculation Black men have endured through slavery and the Jim Crow era. These toxic levels of masculinity expectations include a lack of vulnerability, which is societally defined as feminine, a lack of expressing emotions except for anger, not exploring societally feminine defined hobbies such as ballet or cheerleading.

Black men have no access to femininity according to Afro-Pessimism, which is not true for their white counterparts, and Black men's masculinity is defined as inherently deviant due to their societally dehumanized state of being. For Black men the intersection between gender identity and gender expression means that their masculinity is defined as deviant precisely because they are both Black and men. Typically, being a man invokes privilege in our society but for Black men this is only true intra-communally because other Black people do not see them as inherently deviant. This is because this idea of Black masculinity being assigned as inherently deviant means that institutional racism actually governs both their bodies and choices instead of them and as we know, under anti-Black western society Black men are not men but, deviant objects and thus cannot have privilege in a society that views them this way.

The Black Queer Community and Gender Performance as Safety

The reason that the first Pride, which celebrates the LGBT+ community, was a riot is also the same reason that Black men are targeted by the police: so that Police can uphold and protect the assets of the rich and the interests of heteronormative White society (Dario et al.. 2019; Delgado 2018; Dwyer 2011; Hill 2020; Williams and Murphy 1990). These Black queer experiences are indicators that institutional racism-and White Supremacy will continue to exist if we are not honest about what they mean for us today (Ikuta and Latimer 2021; Schwartz 2017).

Black trans women perfectly, and tragically, epitomize what it is to have intersectional social locations. They simultaneously are ignored, dehumanized, and even brutalized societally, by police, Black people, non-transgender LGBT folks (Serpe and Nadal 2017; Ponton 2016; Schwartz 2020; Ritchie and Jones-Brown 2017).

This context is what informs perspectives such as Drew's and Lamonte who passed for feminine even though they did not identify with this. They, like Black trans women, recognize the danger in being labeled masculine regardless of gender identity. The precarity of Black queer existence is worsened by the community-wide exclusion of them in Black Lives Matter conversations, despite the movement being started by queer Black women, and also the LGBT+ rights movement sidelining issues that are specific to Black queer people only. Black queer people are never truly allowed to live in society as themselves and if they dare to be themselves they may be harmed or rejected by members of society. This is why Drew and Lamonte did not feel allowed to own their autonomy in police interactions by informing them of their gender identity.

Chapter 6: CONCLUSION

My findings for this thesis were that an overwhelming majority of my young Black participants felt that they had no bodily autonomy in the presence of the police and in their everyday lives. This was due to their status as Black people; however, how they experienced this lack of bodily autonomy depended heavily on how their social location as Black people intersected with their other marginalized identities, particularly regarding their gender, sexual orientation, and or gender identity.

Straight Black men experienced their racialized lack of bodily autonomy through not being able to simply be in public spaces and instead having to always be aware of themselves and police at every instant. This awareness of themselves included being aware of their own labeling as deviant which manifested in having to "walk with a purpose", which entailed acting as if one had somewhere to be because the implication is that a non-laboring Black man with free time is suspicious. The straight Black women that I interviewed had to contend with how society has deemed Blackness as inherently emasculating and violent because of that ability to emasculate. These Black women told stories of not being afforded their own complicated dignity as women because they were also Black. This included one participant being suspected of being a sex worker by police as she rode home from the hospital with her uncle. I believe that an experience like that sums up the societal and structural obstacle of inheriting Black womanhood.

Queer Black people, particularly those who were also genderqueer, experienced their lack of bodily autonomy through the gender dysphoria of being misgendered but also not feeling free to be non-heteronormative. Specifically, trans masculine Black young adults spoke of being misgendered as women but also being unsure of which binary gender was more safe in perception as being Black would always be a master status for them due to its overtly and historically assumed innate and inherent deviant nature.

My thesis adds to the theories of Intersectionality and Afro-Pessimism through its specific attention toward and analysis of the heavily stereotyped social location of being Black as it pertains to the *non-monolithic* Black American experience and thus their humanity. This can be seen in how the threat of police brutality impacted the Black participants but how it did so depended on their other marginalized social locations. Black men avoided the threat of police brutality by "walking with a purpose. Black women found themselves vulnerable to police brutality because they lacked the access to femininity, which equates to innocence, that their white peers had. Lastly, Black queer people struggled with being misgendered but also feeling to vulnerable to correct this.

Chapter 7: PUBLIC SOCIOLOGY IMPLICATIONS

Based on the data I collected with this thesis my hope for policy is a future that considers

and understands Intersectionality, that multiple marginalized social locations can impact specific

groups, such as straight Black women, straight Black men, and Black queer people, uniquely. In

addition to this understanding of Intersectionality, this would also include understanding that

anti-blackness is very embedded into our society systemically as viewed through the lens of

Afro-Pessimism.

This thesis was inspired in part by my passion for advocating for structural change in

policing such that young Black people could self-autonomize and self-actualize as full human

beings whose lives matter and have independent meaning. Therefore, the implications of this

research should include more legislation against anti-Black attitudes wherever Black people are

in society and regardless of any other marginalized social locations or memberships in minority

groups. This is why I would like to see a society wide understanding of what it means to have

intersectional social locations, especially within the Black community because with this

understanding could come a more unified Black community. I also believe that one way anti-

Black police brutality could be curbed would be by ending qualified immunity which "protects

police officers from any and all liability in civil suits if their actions do not violate known and

"clearly established" laws (Nemeth 2019).

I believe society's understanding of Intersectionality theory is imperative to Black

people's ability to self-autonomize anywhere and everywhere in society, in the way that white

people are able to, without being limited by normalized racist stereotypes. This is because it is

clear in our society that not understanding Intersectionality at the structural level leads to more

obstacles in life, including in police interactions, for people with intersectional, marginalized

social locations as seen in this thesis by the experiences of young college-educated straight Black women, straight Black men, and Black queer folks. Understanding Intersectionality theory is also important in unifying the Black community more fully. Currently, intra community conversations regarding misogyny, homophobia, and transphobia separate us concretely because non-support is often implied. Black people who invoke these types of bigotry do so by utilizing an us versus them mentality. Black men may frame their misogyny through the lens of being marginalized by their Blackness not recognizing that anti-Blackness is not a monolithic experience. The same can be said for straight Black people, such as Dave Chapelle and his controversial Netflix series, who define the LGBT+ community as privileged white people despite the fact that Black queer people often are the most brutalized in either community. What's missing is the understanding that racism is not monolithic which would enable the possibility of a more universal Black perspective.

I also believe that qualified immunity for police officers should end to combat the systemic way in which Black bodily autonomy is severely limited where police are concerned. The end of qualified immunity would mean providing a possible deterrent for police officers who were previously prone to police brutality. It could also lessen the fear and trauma that Black people experience in police interactions if this deterrent was made real assuming that it would result in less police brutality. Even if the end of qualified immunity did not lessen police brutality against Black people these police officers would be far more likely to be held accountable for their actions without their immunity from this possibility. This is why I see it as most central to specifically Black people's civil rights as it is direct in its social *and* political impact. I see the end of qualified immunity as a civil rights issue because it is that central to the goal of Black people's ability to be free and live freely.

Chapter 8: FUTURE RESEARCH

One factor that I believe is important to future research concerning Black people and their freedom and capacity to act is social media. Much of the Black Lives Matter movement's protest first appeared online before coming into fruition outside of the digital realm. It is there that marginalized individuals get to escape the fear and persecution of their lived realities in order to participate in protest that some of them wouldn't ordinarily be able to. Many of the fifteen participants I interviewed expressed fear of going to protests due to fears about losing their jobs or fears about their safety, but they all said that because of this they put their energies into spreading awareness online. This is because the internet and social media are a place where marginalized people have more ability to be seen and heard being that the physical body is not present. The internet provides marginalized people with the opportunity of parthenogenesis (Russell 2020). One can choose to be who they are or someone else entirely. One can be who they truly are instead of who they pretend to be such as a Black person not having to code switch, which is racial gaslighting because it defines Black people as they are as inherently wrong or unprofessional. Racial gaslighting is defined as "The political, social, economic and cultural process that perpetuates and normalizes a white supremacist reality through pathologizing those who resist (Davis and Ernst 2017)." Also, it is important to note that much of the LGBT+ community relies on the internet to be in community with each other, particularly younger queer people and queer people of color. When a trans person cannot be themselves in the public sphere they can and often do turn to the internet to interact with people who affirm them. When queer youth find themselves isolated in their potentially conservative hometowns they often find other queer youth online instead. These affirmations of LGBT+ people online can be very positive impacts towards one's sense of self-worth which is why apps like TikTok are so popular among these groups. This online world building is an act of defiance against the physical world that wants marginalized folks dead (Wilderson et al.. 2017). This is not hyperbolic. One can even choose to be no one at all and operate under an anonymous alias instead.

I assert that the internet is not an imagined reality. It is an actual reality. The internet is not a social construct though it was created within society it is inherently real (Russell 2020). One has to work to maintain gender, even if you are cisgender, because it is fake. The same is not true for the internet which is the same across countries and cultures though it can be limited (Russell 2020). It is not like money which is also a social construct. How could the internet not be real after events like that of January 6, 2021 in Washington DC where a coup took place that was created and started online, crossing into the physical world only for the event itself after living online for weeks? After this past year where we lived our lives online while we physically were in isolation due to Covid-19?

However, capitalism is poison to this online world and parthenogenesis because it thrives through exploitation. Also, because both gender and race are social constructs they can be used to exploit us. Online this is seen as rich tech conglomerates using our data, the same data we give them to create our online selves, to advertise to us and even to make us feel less secure in ourselves so that we buy these advertised products (Russell 2020).

I believe that future research should include the internet and its pros and cons along with studying Black people and their bodily autonomy and online parthenogenesis.

www.ingramcontent.com/pod-product-compliance
Lightning Source LLC
Chambersburg PA
CBHW072155020426
42334CB00018B/2025